DISCOVER
Butterflies

Contributing writer:
Gary Dunn

Consultant:
Betty Lane Faber, Ph.D.

601302

Publications International, Ltd.

418 7845

Photo Credits:

Front Cover: J. Sainz (center); Susan Middleton: (top & bottom left).

Back Cover: Photo/Nats: Muriel V. Williams

Art Resource: Tutino: 4 (left center); Nimatallah: 5; Scala: 38 (top left); **Comstock:** 18 (top right), 28 (bottom); Gwen Fidler: 13 (center), 35 (top left); Phyllis Greenberg: 39; Russ Kinne: Front endsheet (top right, bottom left & title), 15 (bottom), 22 (center), 24 (top left, center & bottom), 25, 26 (top left & top right), 27 (center), 28 (top & center), 29 (top & center), 30, 34 (left center), 42 (top); George D. Lepp: 12 (top left), 13 (bottom left), 34 (top right & bottom), 37 (top left); Mike & Carol Werner: 33; **Gary A. Dunn:** 18 (center); **Eagle River Media Productions:** J.L. Gressitt: 31 (bottom), 43 (bottom center); Glenn Oliver: 6 (bottom right), 41 (top right & bottom right), back endsheet (top left); **Educational Images, Ltd./Ron West:** 12 (bottom); **Entomological Society of America/Ries Memorial Slide Collection:** 7 (top), 18 (top left), 19 (right center); **FPG International:** Lee Balterman: 42 (center); Dave Gleiter: 13 (bottom); Robert Rathe: 43 (top); Sunni: 11; L. West: 13 (right), 22 (bottom left); **Field Museum of Natural History:** 4 (top left); **Brian Franczak:** 6 (top left); **International Stock Photography:** Steve Myers: 40 (bottom right); Tom & Michele Grimm: 19 (top); **Kenneth Lorenzen:** 9 (top), 20 (top left, top center, top right & bottom center), 21 (top left, top center, top right & bottom center); **Charles W. Melton:** Table of contents (top right), 8 (bottom), 15 (top left), 16 (top left), 19 (top center), 20 (bottom left & bottom right), 22 (top right), 23, 27 (bottom), 32 (top), 36 (bottom), 38 (top right), back endsheet (top right); **Susan Middleton:** Front endsheet (top left), 4 (top right & bottom), 10 (bottom), 16 (bottom), 22 (top right), 26 (center & bottom), 29 (bottom), 31 (top & center), 38 (bottom), back endsheet (left center & bottom right); **Photo/Nats:** Gay Bumgarner: 15 (center), Priscilla Connell: Table of contents (bottom left), 27 (top), 40 (top); Hal Horwitz: 32 (bottom left); John F. O'Connor: 18 (bottom); David M. Stone: 41 (top center), 43 (center); Muriel V. Williams: 17, 21 (bottom left), back endsheet (top); **Gary Retherford:** Front endsheet (top center, left center, right center, bottom center), Table of contents (left center), 7 (center), 8 (top & left center), 9 (right center & bottom), 14 (top left & bottom), 32 (center), 35 (top right & bottom right), 40 (bottom left), back endsheet (top left, right center & bottom left); **J. Sainz:** Front endsheet (bottom right), table of contents (top left & right center), 37 (bottom right); **Gregory K. Scott:** 19 (bottom), 21 (bottom right); **SuperStock:** 10 (top right & left center), 16 (center), 34 (top left), 36 (left center), 38 (right center), 42 (bottom left & bottom center), Herbert Lanks: 36 (top); **The Wildlife Collection:** 7 (bottom); 24 (top right), 32 (bottom right).

Illustrations: Pablo Montes O'Neill; Lorie Robare

Contributing writer Gary Dunn has been an entomologist for many years. He was an extension entomologist at Michigan State University for 11 years, during which time he worked in their entomology youth education program. Mr. Dunn served as the advisor for the Young Entomologists Society for five years; he is currently their executive director and editor of their three magazines, Insect World, Y.E.S. Quarterly, and Flea Market. Mr. Dunn has appeared often on television and radio talk shows. He especially enjoys visiting schools with his traveling bug zoo.

Consultant Dr. Betty Lane Faber holds a Ph.D. in entomology from Rutgers University. She is currently affiliated with the Douglass Project for Rutgers Women in Math, Science, and Engineering. Among her many professional accomplishments, Dr. Faber finds that she has especially enjoyed working with children. She has taught children's workshops for the American Museum of Natural History and has participated in the New York Academy of Sciences' Scientists-in-Schools program. She was also the head nature specialist for three years at Harbor Hill Day Camp in Mount Freedom, New Jersey, where she helped campers catch, observe, and enjoy insects of all kinds.

CONTENTS

THE FIRST BUTTERFLIES

appeared on earth about 75 million years ago. Dinosaurs and butterflies lived together

for at least 10 million years—and then the dinosaurs became extinct. It would be another 25 million years before the first humans walked the land. Scientists believe that butterflies have existed in their present form for the past 50 million years.

Butterflies are painted on the walls of ancient Egyptian tombs. They adorn early Chinese

pottery. The Romans were fascinated by them and called them *papilio*. And though people have wondered about the butterfly for thousands of years, we have only studied them for two centuries. Lepidopterists—those who study butterflies and moths—now know many facts about butterfly life cycles, feeding and mating habits, migration, and body structures.

THE FIRST BUTTERFLIES

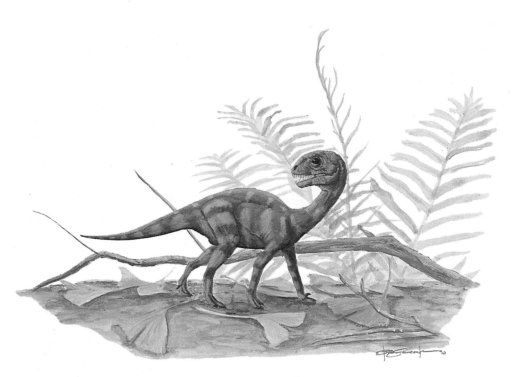

The first moths and butterflies shared the land with dinosaurs and other prehistoric animals.

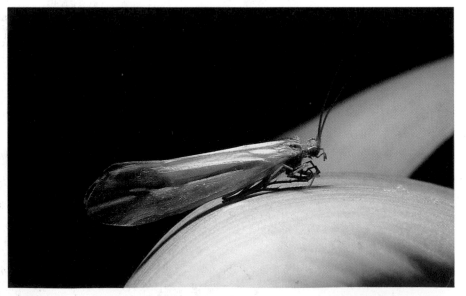

Caddisflies have remained nearly unchanged since prehistoric days. The first butterflies were relatives of some early caddisflies that had hairy wings.

The story of the butterfly began about 140 million years ago. At that time, dinosaurs walked the land and swam in the sea. The earth was covered with many strange and different-looking plants and animals. It would be at least 75 million years before the dinosaurs disappeared.

Giant reptiles were not the only animals that lived on the earth. There were many small animals, too. Most of these small animals were insects. All of the insects we see today came from these insects of long ago.

Among these prehistoric insects was one that had wings covered with hair. These were the caddisflies. Some kinds of caddisflies can still be found today. Some of the hairy-winged caddisflies changed into the insect we now call the butterfly. Then, as now, baby caddisflies lived in the water. They have always had a special ability to make silk threads, which they use to net insects and small fish for food. Some of the young caddisflies of long ago probably started to spend some of their time on land, feeding on tender green leaves. Because they didn't have to share their food with so many other caddisflies, they had a good chance of growing up. The adult caddisflies were weak fliers, so they hid during the day when other animals were looking for food. They waited until dark before becoming active.

After millions of years, these special land caddisflies became the first moths. These first moths looked different from their caddisfly relatives. Their wings were covered with colored flat hairs, called scales. But like caddisflies, they flew at night and hid during the day. As time went by, some of the moths started visiting flowers during the day. These moths were more brightly colored than the ones that hid during the daytime. There are still day-flying moths in many parts of the world today.

The first real butterflies appeared about 50 million years ago. They were born of the day-flying moths. Their wings were large, and patterned in white, brown, and black. They looked very much like the swallowtail butterflies of today. After many more years, other colors started to appear on the wings and bodies of butterflies. These new colors helped the butterflies protect themselves from birds and other animals. By blending with their surroundings, butterflies could now fly around during the daytime and not become an easy meal for some other animal. Butterflies had become one of the most beautiful—and successful—kinds of insects.

How do we know so much about the history of butterflies? Scientists have studied their history through the fossils of caddisflies, moths, and butterflies. The oldest known butterfly fossil is 40 million years old. This fossil has given us important information about the origin of butterflies.

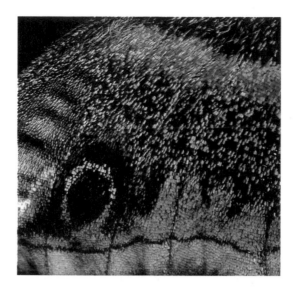

As the years passed, the hair on the day-flying moths' wings became colorful scales.

Some day-flying moths look enough like butterflies to confuse even an expert butterfly watcher! This day-flying moth is a tiger moth. Predators may not want to eat it—it looks like a bad-tasting butterfly.

Prehistoric butterflies are thought to have looked much like swallowtails found today.

THE FIRST BUTTERFLIES

The largest butterflies are found high in the treetops of the tropical rain forest. Many of these butterflies never come close to the ground, for food is plentiful in the canopy of the forest.

Today, butterflies are found just about everywhere you can imagine. They can be found at the north pole and on mountaintops. They live in forests, deserts, and jungles. They have even been found flying over oceans as they travel from country to country! The only place where butterflies do not live is in Antarctica, near the South Pole. Butterflies are least common where the weather is cold and most common where the weather is warm. Warm weather gives them lots of time to grow. It is hottest at the earth's equator. The steamy jungle is where the most—and the biggest—butterflies are found.

Butterflies and moths are the only insects with colorful scales on their bodies and wings.

Insects are the most common animals in the world. Three out of every four animals is some kind of insect. Beetles, butterflies, moths, ants, bees,

flies, grasshoppers, cockroaches, praying mantids, and dragonflies are all insects. Almost half of the insects are beetles. Butterflies and moths are the second largest insect group. All of the other insect groups are much less common.

Butterflies and moths have a long, hollow tongue called a "proboscis." The proboscis is kept coiled like a garden hose when it is not being used to sip nectar from flowers.

The bodies and wings of butterflies and moths are covered with colorful scales. The dust on your fingers after touching a butterfly or moth are some of the scales that have rubbed off. Butterflies and moths also have a very special tongue called a proboscis. This tongue is hollow, like a soda straw, and is used to drink nectar from flowers.

Butterflies and moths are very similar, so they belong to the same insect group. You can tell a butterfly from a moth in a number of ways. First, butterflies are usually more colorful than moths. Butterflies may be patterned in red, orange, yellow, green, blue, purple, or silver. Moths are usually plain gray or brown. Secondly, butterflies hold their wings straight up when resting. Moths fold their wings flat over their backs. Thirdly, butterfly antennae are skinny with little knobs  at the tips. Moth antennae are either feathery or they are skinny without any knobs. And last, butterflies are active during the day, while moths are more active at night.

Skippers are insects that seem to be half moth and half butterfly. Their bodies are large and mothlike, and their wings are often dull, like moth wings. Skippers are active during the day, though, and their wings may be colorful. Their antennae are more like a butterfly's, though. They are hooked instead of knobbed at the ends. Experts often disagree as to how skippers should be grouped. In this book, they are grouped with the butterflies.

Most of the butterflies and moths in your neighborhood can be told apart by their colors and by the time of day—or night—they are active. There are some day-flying moths and some plainly colored butterflies, though. You might be fooled once in awhile! But don't let it bother you. Even a well-trained butterfly watcher may be taught a lesson by these unusual butterflies and moths.

This lawn skipper may be confused with a moth. Its body is large and hairy like a moth's, and it folds its wings like a moth when it rests. Its antennae are more like a butterfly's, though; they are not feathered like a moth's antennae.

The day-flying Uranus moth (right) looks like a swallowtail butterfly. Thousands of these moths (above) are swarming about flowering trees in Costa Rica.

Butterflies and moths form the second largest group of insects. Only beetles form a larger group.

9

BUTTERFLY BODIES

come in all shapes and sizes. In fact, of the 20,000 kinds of butterflies, no two look exactly alike. Butterflies range in size from the tiny dwarf blue butterfly— with its half-inch wingspread—to the giant Queen Alexandra birdwing that has a wingspread of 13 inches!

Butterflies have unique shapes and colors that help them survive in a special habitat. A butterfly may look like a dry, brown leaf or the rough bark of a tree. Some butterflies wear warning colors or patterns that say, "I'm poisonous!" Still others "pretend" to be dangerous, taking on the appearance of hornets or poisonous butterflies. Though they look different, all butterflies have some things in common. All have a three-part body, six legs, a set of antennae, and, of course, wings.

BUTTERFLY BODIES

The middle part of the butterfly is called the thorax. Inside the thorax are strong muscles that move the wings and legs.

The coiled proboscis and wing scales separate butterflies from the rest of the insects in the world.

Quite a bit of a butterfly's head is covered with its huge compound eyes. This close-up shows both its eyes and its coiled proboscis. To feed, the butterfly uncoils its proboscis and uses it like a soda straw to sip nectar from flowers.

Many people think that insects are "yucky" and that butterflies are beautiful. It is easy to forget that butterflies are insects. We know this because insects' bodies are all built in a similar way. None of the insects, including butterflies, have bones inside their bodies. It is the outer shell of their body that acts as their skeleton. Like the other insects, butterflies have three pairs of legs, three body parts—head, thorax, and abdomen—and one pair of antennae attached to the head. Butterflies are different from other insects because they have a coiled proboscis and colored scales on their wings and bodies.

The butterfly head is located at the front of the body. Most of the butterfly's face is covered with its two large eyes. These eyes are "compound" eyes—not single eyeballs like ours. Each compound eye is made up of many eyeballs grouped together. There may be as few as 50 or as many as 20,000 individual eyeballs in an insect's compound eye. Each little eyeball sees a small part of what the butterfly is looking at. Together, the group of eyeballs makes it a picture.

Unlike some animals, butterflies are able to see colors. This is important because different kinds of butterflies need to find flowers of certain colors. Butterflies can also see movement and shapes. This helps them find food and other butterflies. It also helps them avoid enemies.

A pair of antennae is connected to the top of the butterfly's head, between the compound eyes. The antennae are sometimes called "feelers" but they are used for much more than feeling. They are also used for smelling and hearing! The antennae are long and slender, and are knobbed at the tips.

The mouthparts of the butterfly are attached to the lower front part of the head. The mouthparts are made up of the coiled proboscis and two furry, fingerlike lips.

Behind the head, in the middle of the butterfly, is the thorax. The four wings and six legs are all attached here. The inside of the thorax is filled with strong muscles that move the wings and legs. The legs are each divided into five parts and have little hooks on their feet for grasping. Butterflies can taste their food with their feet! The members of one group of butterflies have front legs that are small and brushlike. These "brush-footed" butterflies stand on only four legs.

Most butterflies stand on six legs. But a small group of "brush-footed" butterflies stand on only four legs.

Butterflies can taste with their feet! Small pores—tiny holes—on their feet pick up the "flavor" of the thing on which they are standing. The pores trigger sensory nerves that tell the butterfly's brain whether or not the thing is good to eat.

BUTTERFLY BODIES

Seen from above, this giant swallowtail will blend with the ground and vegetation below.

The pattern on top of a butterfly's wings is usually different from the pattern underneath.

Seen from below, the giant swallowtail will blend with sky and sun above.

Butterflies have four wings. The front pair are usually larger than the back pair but they move together when the butterfly is flying. The shape of the wings has a lot to do with the way a butterfly flies. Butterflies with long, narrow wings fly fast and can change direction quickly. The fastest butterflies are able to fly at a speed of nearly 20 miles per hour! Butterflies with large, broad wings are able to float and glide through the air over long distances.

Each butterfly wing has a dozen or more veins that carry the flow of blood and air into the wings. They also make the wings more sturdy. The wings are covered with colored scales on both the top and bottom surfaces. Each scale is attached to the wing by a narrow stalk. The scales overlap one another like the shingles on the roof of a house. Each wing of a butterfly holds thousands of scales. And in the case of a large butterfly, like the monarch, each wing may be covered with nearly half a million scales!

The color patterns found on a butterfly's wings are usually important to that butterfly's way of life. They can camouflage, soak up the warm sun, scare away hungry birds, or help attract a mate. Some color patterns have shapes that look like letters or numbers. Every letter of the alphabet and all ten numerals have been found between butterflies and moths!

If you handle a butterfly, you'll find that the scales are easily rubbed off. Losing a small number of scales is no problem for most butterflies. But the loss of many scales from one wing can cripple a butterfly. Not all butterflies' wings are covered with scales. The glass-wing butterflies of South America have scales along their veins only. You can see right through the rest of the wing!

The long part of the body behind the thorax is called the abdomen. If you look closely, you will see that it is divided into sections. This makes it easier for a butterfly to wiggle its abdomen, just as our skeletons are jointed so we can move. Inside the abdomen is the butterfly's heart, stomach, and other organs.

Butterflies do not breathe through the mouth and they do not have noses or lungs. Instead, the air gets into the body through holes in the sides of the abdomen. When air enters these breathing holes, it travels through a system of tiny tubes to all parts of the body. The abdomen—and all other parts of the body—are filled with blood. Butterfly blood may be yellow, brown, or green in color, but it is never red like human blood.

It may be hard to believe, but out of 20,000 different kinds of butterflies, no two kinds look exactly alike. But this isn't even the full story. Most female butterflies are different, in size and color, from males of their species. Also, many butterflies in the same species are colored differently depending on the time of the year and where they live. With these extra differences it looks more like there are 50,000 different kinds of beautiful butterflies!

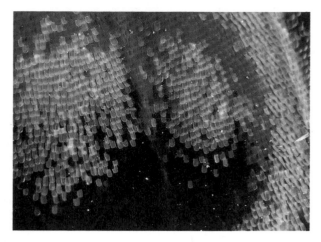

The scales on a butterfly's wings overlap each other like the shingles on the roof of a house. This is a close-up of the wing of a buckeye butterfly.

Be gentle! The loss of too many scales can cripple a butterfly.

Scales that have rubbed off on your fingers may feel buttery. Perhaps this is how the butterfly got its name.

Gulf fritillary

A BUTTERFLY'S LIFE

is a thing of wonder. From egg to caterpillar to chrysalis to a butterfly that will lay more eggs, a butterfly has four life stages.

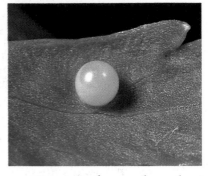

A butterfly's life is also full of danger. The moment it is laid as an egg, it is a possible meal for birds and other small animals. Once hatched, it must find enough food to eat and still stay safe from predators. While feeding, the caterpillar may be a victim of artificial or natural poisons. Then, in its "mummy" stage it must survive wind, weather, and more predators. If all goes well, the new butterfly emerges and spreads its wings! There is no time to

rest, though. The butterfly must now avoid enemies, find food, and mate—so the cycle can go on and on.

A BUTTERFLY'S LIFE

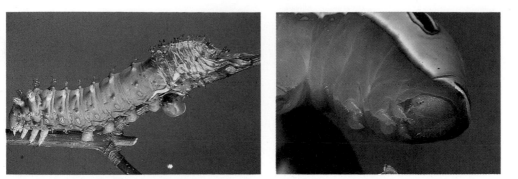

The caterpillar on the left is shedding its skin. Its tail end is not yet free of the old skin. The close-up on the right shows the head of a swallowtail caterpillar. You may be able to see its eyes and mouthparts as well as its six legs, which are attached to its thorax. The markings on top of its body are "false eyes" that help to scare enemies.

A butterfly starts life as an egg that was laid by an adult female butterfly. In its second stage, a tiny caterpillar hatches from the egg and it begins to eat as well as grow. A caterpillar grows by shedding its outside skeleton and making a new, larger one. The old skeleton splits down the back and the caterpillar wriggles its way out. There is a very thin skin under the skeleton that keeps the caterpillar from "falling apart." This skin also makes a liquid "cement" that coats the caterpillar's body. This cement will form the new outer skeleton. But before the cement has hardened, the caterpillar fills itself with air and stretches the new skeleton. It grows to fit the larger size.

After shedding its skeleton about six times, the caterpillar turns into a chrysalis. Inside the chrysalis, the caterpillar is changing shape. When the change is complete, the butterfly will push its way out of the chrysalis and crawl free. A butterfly does not shed its skeleton, so once a caterpillar becomes a butterfly it will not grow any bigger. Small butterflies do not grow up to be big butterflies.

Although they grow to be butterflies, caterpillars do not look much like butterflies. Caterpillars do have a head, thorax, and abdomen like all insects. But there are no compound eyes on the caterpillar's head. Instead, there are six single eyeballs on each side of the caterpillar's head. These eyes cannot see colors, but they can see some movement and shapes. Caterpillars also have two antennae, but they are short and without knobs at the ends. The caterpillar's mouth-

In a butterfly's first life stage, it may not even be recognized as a butterfly.

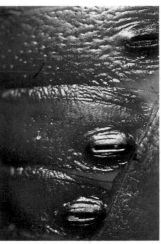

This is a close up look at the breathing holes on a caterpillar's abdomen. These holes are known as "spiracles."

Birds, mice, spiders, and some insects eat caterpillars. Canned caterpillars are even sold in Mexico as human food!

18

parts are found on the lower front part of the head, but instead of the coiled proboscis, there are two strong jaws. These jaws are perfect for chewing the leaves and other plant parts that are the caterpillar's food. A coiled proboscis would be of no use to a caterpillar!

The caterpillar's thorax has six legs attached to it, just like the thorax of all other insects. Each leg is jointed, and is divided into five sections. There is a claw at the end of each leg. The caterpillar uses its legs for crawling and for holding pieces of plant while eating. A caterpillar, of course, does not have wings on its thorax.

The abdomen is the longest part of a caterpillar's body. It is divided into 10 sections. This makes it easier for the caterpillar to wriggle and move. Inside the abdomen are muscles, a heart, and a stomach. The abdomen—and the rest of the body—is filled with insect blood, just like butterflies. On each side of the abdomen there are about eight breathing holes.

There are several pairs of "false legs" on the underside of a caterpillar's abdomen. These legs are fatter than the real legs. The false legs have rows of tiny hooks on them. They are useful for crawling and clinging to branches or leaves.

If caterpillars do not have wings to fly away, how do they protect themselves? Some caterpillars are disguised to look like twigs, bark, or bird droppings—things that are not good to eat. There are even some caterpillars that eat poisonous plants, like milkweed, so that they taste bad.

The female butterfly lays her eggs on the right kind of plant so the just-hatched caterpillars will have food right away. Most caterpillars can eat only one or two kinds of plants.

Butterfly eggs are quite small. Some are only a little larger than the head of a pin. (These are magnified many times.) Butterfly eggs may be round, domed, egg-shaped, or sausage-shaped.

With any luck, this caterpillar's enemies will not be able to tell it apart from the twig on which it rests. Can you tell the twig and caterpillar apart?

A BUTTERFLY'S LIFE

The monarch caterpillar grows as it eats milkweed plants. It outgrows its skeleton about six times.

When the caterpillar sheds its skeleton for the last time, it attaches itself to a branch with silk threads.

The caterpillar now begins to change into a chrysalis. It may take as long as a day for the change to occur.

It soon becomes apparent that great changes have taken place inside the chrysalis.

The shell of the chrysalis is now clear enough to see the adult butterfly inside. It won't be long now!

When it is time to emerge, the butterfly pumps fluid into its head and thorax. This helps split the chrysalis open.

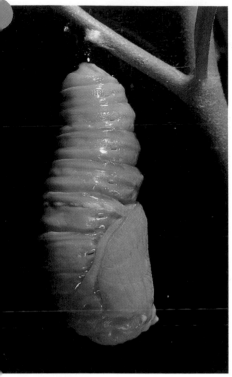

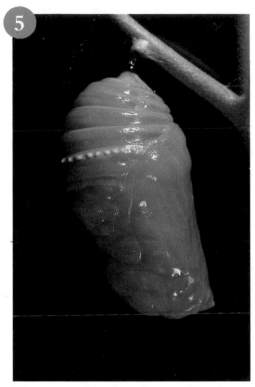

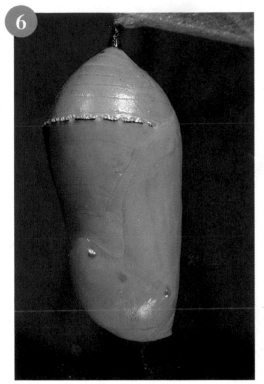

side the chrysalis, the caterpillar rns to "jelly." This jelly has all the lls needed to build a butterfly.

The monarch's chrysalis may blend with its host plant, but many predators will leave it alone anyway. They know it tastes awful!

The living creature inside the chrysalis produces waste, which stays inside until the butterfly emerges.

he new butterfly hangs from its rysalis while blood pumps into its ings. This makes its wings unfold to eir full size.

The butterfly's wings   must dry for about an hour before   it can fly. At this time, waste drips from the tip of its abdomen.

The adult monarch may live for 10 months before dying of old age. This is a very long life for a butterfly!

21

SORTING OUT BUTTERFLIES

is quite a challenge! There are over 20,000 kinds of butterflies in the world. Not only that, butterflies are related to moths and skippers, as well. Together, all three are known as Lepidoptera, a word made of the Latin words lepido and ptera, meaning "scale" and "wing." "Scaly wings" are unique to these insects alone. There may be over 165,000 kinds of Lepidoptera!

But within the order—or group—called Lepidoptera, butterflies can be sorted by species. Butterflies that share important things like body size or wing shape may be placed in the same species. By sorting butterflies into groups we can better understand how they have lived and spread to habitats all over the world.

SORTING OUT BUTTERFLIES

Wood nymph

Little wood satyr

Brown

Ringlet

All animals, including insects, can be sorted into groups according to the ways they are alike and the ways they are different. The butterfly and moth group is known as the Lepidoptera. Butterflies and moths can be further separated into two groups by differences in their antennae, the way they hold their wings, their wing color, and the time of day they are active. When this is done, we find there are about 20,000 different kinds of butterflies and 145,000 different kinds of moths in the world.

By looking even closer at the butterflies, we find they can be divided into 15 smaller groups, or "families." Scientists have given each butterfly family its own special name. Each family has a "common" name as well as a Latin name. These names are recognized and used by butterfly watchers all over the world.

Wood Nymphs, Satyrs, Browns, and Ringlets • *Satyridae*

These small-to-medium-size butterflies can be found all around the world. It is a large family with close to 3,000 different kinds. Most of these butterflies are whitish, brownish, or tan in color with eye spots on the wings. Most of these butterflies stay very near the place where they emerged from the chrysalis. They are common in meadows, forest clearings, mountaintops, and jungles. They seldom fly very far from vegetation. Their favorite means of escape is to suddenly disappear into the bushes or drop to the ground and hide in the leaves.

Owls • *Brassolidae*

Owl butterflies are large butterflies that are found only in the jungles of Central and South America. They have broad wings and large black-ringed yellow spots on the undersides of their hind wings. When their wings are spread, the pattern looks like an owl. This probably scares away enemies and helps protect them. Owl butterflies are strong fliers. They are active at sunrise and again at sunset. They feed on overripe fruit and are easily attracted to baits made of mashed fruit.

Owl

Skippers and Duskywings • *Hesperiidae*

There are almost 3,000 different kinds of skippers. They can be found in all parts of the world. They are small or medium-size butterflies with large, mothlike bodies, and short wings. Their antennae are hooked at the tip. Most skippers are brown, red-brown, orange, or tan in color. Many of them have white or silver markings on their wings. Their flight is short, fast, and uneven. When they rest, they fold their wings flat over their back, as do moths.

Skipper

Giant Skippers • *Megathymidae*

Giant skippers are large butterflies with wingspreads of nearly three inches. There are only about 50 kinds of giant skippers; most are found in the southwestern United States and in Mexico. They have big, heavy bodies but they can still fly very fast. When resting, these skippers hold their wings straight up over their back.

Giant Skipper

25

SORTING OUT BUTTERFLIES

Snout

White

Yellow

Orangetip

Snouts • *Libytheidae*
This small group of unusual butterflies is found in many areas of the world. There are only 10 kinds of snout butterflies known. The Bachman's snout butterfly lives in the southwestern United States. They are called snout butterflies because the shape of their face is long and pointed. They are strong, fast fliers. Some snout butterflies have mass migrations that fill the skies with billions of butterflies.

Whites, Yellows, Sulphurs, and Orangetips • *Pieridae*
Many of the 2,000 members of this butterfly family are named for the color of their wings, like the great southern white, Sara orangetip, and little yellow. One of these bright yellow butterflies may have inspired the named "butterfly." These medium-size butterflies are found in all parts of the world, even in areas close to the North Pole. Most of the caterpillars of these butterflies feed on pea, bean, cabbage, broccoli, and similar plants. They can be pests in gardens! The common cabbage white can be found just about everywhere in the world where these kinds of plants are grown for food.

Some of the butterflies in this family have occasional mass migrations. Their flight is rapid and close to the ground. People who have seen these swarms of white butterflies say it looks like a snowstorm!

Anglewings, Admirals, and Fritillaries (Brush-footed Butterflies) • *Nymphalidae*

There are over 3,000 kinds of butterflies in this family, which makes it the largest butterfly family. They are found all over the world. They are active on bright, sunny days and spend lots of time visiting flowers. They can often be seen sunning themselves with their wings stretched out.

These butterflies have small, stunted front legs that look like brushes. Because of these "brush feet," the butterflies stand on four legs, not six. The upper surfaces of their wings are very colorful, but the undersides are plain. The butterflies blend with their surroundings when they are resting, with their wings folded up over their back.

The leaf butterflies are champions of disguise. Their wings are brilliant orange-brown or blue on top, but the undersides look just like a leaf. These "leaves" are complete with a stem, veins, and silver spots that look like little holes! Some brush-footed butterflies, like the red admiral and painted lady, are migratory. They travel great distances each spring.

The clicking butterflies of South America make a loud clicking sound with their wings. At first it was thought that the clicking sound was meant to frighten away enemies. We now know that these butterflies protect a small territory and that they chase away other clicking butterflies by making this noise.

Anglewing

Admiral

Gulf fritillary

SORTING OUT BUTTERFLIES

Emperor

Lange's metalmark

Morpho

Emperors • *Apaturidae*
Emperor butterflies fly very fast and they rarely visit flowers. Instead, they get their food from dead animals, manure, rotting fruit, and tree sap. Many emperor butterflies have brilliant, shiny blue wings. Even though they are smaller, some emperors are more beautiful than the morpho butterflies. Emperors are found in all parts of the world. Many emperors are rare and in need of protection.

Metalmarks • *Riodinidae*
These small and medium-size butterflies are found in many parts of the world, including North America. There are several hundred different kinds of metalmarks commonly found in South America. Their common name comes from the shiny, metallic markings on their wings. The South American metalmarks are more colorful than those found in North America. Many metalmarks are able to land on the underside of a leaf when seeking a hiding place.

Morphos • *Morphidae*
Morpho butterflies are known for their large size and brilliant blue wings. All of the morphos have shiny, iridescent blue patches on their wings. Sometimes the whole wing is an iridescent blue. Morpho butterflies are found in South America, Africa, and Asia. They are most active in the early morning and late afternoon. These extremely shy, strong fliers are very difficult to catch as they fly through the jungle. They can be attracted to baits made of mashed fruit, though, and some kinds have become rare because they have been over-collected.

Heliconians and Longwings • *Heliconiidae*

This small group of butterflies is found only in Central America, South America, and the southeastern United States. The caterpillars of these butterflies feed on passionflowers, which are poisonous plants. The poison does not harm the caterpillar. Instead, it is passed on to the chrysalis and the adult butterfly. It actually helps protect all three life stages of the butterfly from enemies! Lizards and birds learn to avoid these caterpillars and butterflies because they taste bad. Heliconians have a slow, lazy flight. They also gather in large groups, called roosts, to spend the night together.

Milkweeds • *Danaidae*

These butterflies are most common in warm parts of Africa and Asia, but there are a few kinds in North and South America. They are medium-size or large. Their front legs are small and stunted. The caterpillars of these butterflies feed on different kinds of milkweed and dogbane plants. These plants contain poisons that make the caterpillars, chrysalids, and butterflies taste bad to birds and other animals. Most of the butterflies in this groups are brilliantly colored in orange and black to help birds remember that they taste bad. Their color patterns are copied by many other non-poisonous butterflies in other families.

Heliconian

Longwing

Milkweed (Monarch)

SORTING OUT BUTTERFLIES

Bog copper

Blue

Glassywing

Harvesters, Hairstreaks, Coppers, and Blues (Gossamer-winged Butterflies) • *Lycaenidae*

There are several thousand different kinds of these small butterflies, and they are found all over the world. The world's smallest butterfly—the pygmy blue of North America with a wingspread of less than one half of an inch—is a member of this family. The upper surface of this family's wings are mostly blue, green, brown, orange, or red. The undersides are usually white, gray, tan, pale green, or pale blue. Gossamer-winged butterflies are most active on sunny days and quickly go into hiding when clouds cover the sun. They are some of the earliest butterflies to fly in the spring. In warm climates, there may be three or more broods during a single season.

The caterpillars of these butterflies often live within colonies of ants, aphids, or leafhoppers where they feed on the young of these insects. Some of these caterpillars are known to eat their own kind!

Mimics and Glassywings • *Ithomiidae*

These medium-size butterflies are found mostly in South America. They have a slow, gliding flight. The mimic butterflies have wing patterns of yellow and black or orange-brown and black. They are poisonous and very bad-tasting to birds and lizards. Glassywing butterflies' wings are covered with only a few scales—you can see right through them.

Swallowtails, Parnassians, and Birdwings • *Papilionidae*

There are about 500 kinds of swallowtail butterflies. They can be found all over the world. Many of them are very large and colorful. The kite swallowtails have the longest wings of any swallowtails. Their "tails" are twice as long as their body. Many swallowtails do not have tails on their hind wings. Swallowtails are strong, fast fliers. They commonly visit flowers in the morning.

Parnassian butterflies live in mountain areas of Europe, Asia, and the North American west. Most have thinly scaled, pale wings—white, yellow, or tan—with red and black "eye spots."

Birdwing butterflies are found in the jungles of India, Southeast Asia, and Papua New Guinea, which is an island near Australia. Birdwings have long, narrow wings with shiny patches of green, yellow, or blue. Their flight is fast and powerful and they stay high among the jungle trees, rarely coming near the ground. Because they are difficult to catch, the first collectors used shotguns to knock them out of the air so that they could be studied. The Queen Alexandra birdwing is the world's largest butterfly. Females have a wingspread of 13 inches! Birdwings are rare and endangered. Some are protected by law, so they may be saved from extinction.

Swallowtail

Parnassian

Birdwing

31

THE WAY A BUTTERFLY ACTS

says a lot about what kind of butterfly it is. Every kind of butterfly has a different way of behaving, because every kind of butterfly has different needs. A butterfly does what it must to meet its special needs. By watching carefully, you will be able to tell kinds of butterflies apart.

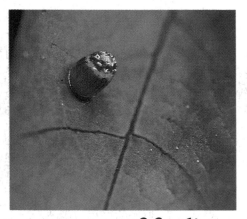

Some butterflies will lay their eggs on only one kind of leaf. This way, the young caterpillars will have the right kind of food to eat. "Tasty" butterflies fly differently than poisonous butterflies. And each kind of butterfly has its own special way of finding a mate. And perhaps most fascinating are the ways some butterflies escape danger.

THE WAY A BUTTERFLY ACTS

Some people can tell butterflies apart by watching the way they fly. The wood satyr (left) has a bolder flight pattern than the skittish little skipper (above).

The behavior of some butterflies is so special that you can easily recognize them from a distance. The way a butterfly flies is a perfect example. Skippers and many brush-footed butterflies are always in a hurry. Satyrs look like they're nervous and afraid to come into the open. Butterflies that taste bad fly boldly in open places with slow, lazy strokes. The ways that different butterflies feed, rest, and protect themselves are also very special.

Caterpillars eat so that they will grow bigger. Caterpillars have an easy time finding their food. The mother butterfly will have carefully laid her eggs on the right kind of plant so that the caterpillars will have plenty to eat. Butterflies eat so that they have energy to fly and to keep warm. They need to spend a lot of their time flying around to find food. They will spend at least half of their day looking for food. They locate flowering plants with the help of their eyes and their antennae.

The female cabbage white butterfly lays her eggs on cabbage, cauliflower, or broccoli. The caterpillars that hatch can be pests.

This butterfly is "puddling." When many butterflies group at a puddle, they are called a "mud-puddle club."

Many butterflies also need drinking water. They may gather in large groups on wet sand or stones to drink water or to feed on salts in the soil. These large groups may hold hundreds of butterflies. Sometimes they are all one kind of butterfly, and sometimes they are many different kinds. These gatherings have been nicknamed "mud-puddle clubs." If you approach the mud-puddle club slowly, it may be possible to get within an arm's length of the butterflies. Butterflies love salt so much, you may be able to get one to drink sweat from your finger or the tip of your nose!

Butterflies are not able to protect themselves by stinging or biting, like many insects. They have to protect themselves in other ways. To protect their eggs, mother butterflies hide them in rough tree bark, flower buds, or on the undersides of leaves.

Once out of the egg shell, caterpillars must defend themselves. Some feed under the cover of night and hide during the day. Others live in groups and wriggle with a force great enough to scare a nearby bird. Some caterpillars are covered with hairs or sharp spines; some have "horns" that are covered with a foul-smelling liquid. A few caterpillars have large, false "eye" spots on their bodies that make them look fearsome.

Some caterpillars feed on plants that are poisonous. The plants do not harm the caterpillars, but the poison makes them taste bad. Birds and other animals that try to eat these caterpillars get a real surprise—and sometimes a stomachache! Most of these bad-tasting caterpillars are brightly colored in red, orange, yellow, and black. These "warning colors" help enemies remember to stay away.

Butterfly chrysalids cannot move to escape from their enemies. They depend on camouflage for protection. They fool their enemies with disguises that make them look like something else—a seed pod, leaf, thorn, twig, or even bird droppings.

Most butterflies can escape from their enemies by flying away. But this doesn't always work, for birds can fly, too! Butterflies' wing scales sometimes

Though this saddleback caterpillar (left) will turn into a moth, it is a good example of how some caterpillars—of butterflies and moths alike—wear poisonous spines for protection. The caterpillar below has false eyes on top of its body.

Slow-moving caterpillars protect themselves in many ways.

This giant swallowtail caterpillar looks like bird droppings. A hungry bird will probably not look at it twice!

THE WAY A BUTTERFLY ACTS

This owl butterfly (right) is one of several butterflies that wear false eyes on their wings. A bird may think the eyes belong to a cat or other large animal.

Would you be surprised if one of the dead leaves of this plant suddenly flew away? The dead-leaf butterfly wears a perfect disguise!

Viceroy

The good-tasting viceroy looks so much like the bad-tasting monarch, predators leave it alone.

Monarch

help them escape from birds. Their scales come off easily, allowing the butterfly to free its wing from a bird's beak. It is like the "tear-away" shirt a football player wears—it is better to have a torn shirt than be tackled!

Some butterflies have "eye" spots or tails on their back wings. These markings confuse birds and get them to aim for the wings and not the butterfly's body. A V-shaped notch in the edge of a butterfly's wing is proof that the butterfly has escaped from a hungry bird's beak.

Many brush-footed butterflies have bright colors and eye spots on the tops of their wings, and gray or brown speckles underneath. When these butterflies land on a tree trunk, a rock, or the ground, they fold their wings and disappear. If a curious bird gets too close, the butterfly opens its wings with a flash of bright color that scares the bird! The butterfly can make a clean getaway.

Some butterflies have wings that are perfect copies of a leaf. Leaf butterflies are green or brown. Some even have black or silver spots that make the "leaf" look like it has been eaten by bugs.

Some butterflies have poisons in their bodies—eaten by the caterpillars and passed on through the chrysalids—that make them taste bad to birds. Like the poisonous caterpillars, these butterflies are also brightly colored in yellow, orange, red, and black. These warning colors work so well that good-tasting butterflies of the same colors are not bothered by birds!

Winter is a dangerous time of the year for many butterflies because of the cold temperatures and the lack of food. Most butterflies spend the winter in hibernation. Hibernation is a sort of "sleep." The cold weather causes a hibernating animal's heartbeat and breathing to become very slow. They burn so little energy that they do not need to eat food. Hibernation can take place in any of the four life stages of a butterfly—egg, caterpillar, chrysalis, or butterfly—depending on the kind of butterfly. It always takes place in the same stage for butterflies of the same kind.

When the weather turns cold, caterpillars and butterflies look for places to spend the winter. They may choose a cave, hollow tree, a building, or simply hide under fallen leaves. Some caterpillars become chrysalids before it gets too cold. The butterflies will come out the following spring. Some butterflies lay their eggs at the end of summer; the caterpillars will hatch in the spring.

Some butterflies migrate—or travel—from one area to another at certain times. Most migratory butterflies move away from the equator in the spring and toward it in the fall. Many butterfly migrations are only in one direction. The purpose for this kind of travel is to find new places to live. Some migrating butterflies, like the monarch and the painted lady, are known to fly more than 1,000 miles in a single trip. Crossing oceans is no problem for them. Painted ladies regularly fly from north Africa to Europe each year.

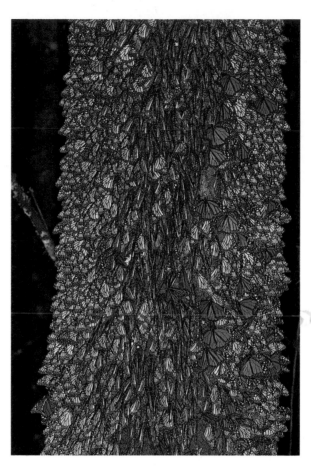

Millions and millions of hibernating monarchs hang from the trees after they have migrated to Pacific Grove, California, or to the mountains outside of Mexico City, Mexico. They will have arrived there in the fall and will leave in the spring. The females will leave eggs on milkweed plants as they make the trip "home."

Butterflies are cold-blooded. If it is a cool day, the butterfly must warm its flight muscles before it flies. The best way is to let its wings soak up the warmth of the sun.

Butterflies that do not migrate must look for a protected place to spend the winter. A hollow tree is a frequent choice.

ARE BUTTERFLIES IMPORTANT?

We agree they add beauty to our world by just being here, but they have added beauty and wonder to our world in many other ways, too. Through the centuries, butterfly wings have been part of jewelry and art. The butterfly has been drawn, painted, and sculpted since time began. And the metamorphosis of the butterfly has become a symbol for life change in stories, poetry, song, and dance.

Butterflies should not be treasured for beauty alone. This colorful, graceful insect is a very important thread in the web of life. For millions of years, the butterfly has been relating to animal and plant life alike. After all this time, it is a shame that we have let some of these insects become endangered and extinct.

ARE BUTTERFLIES IMPORTANT?

When asked to name an insect that helps pollinate flowers, we usually think of bees first. Butterflies may actually pollinate more plants than bees, though!

Butterflies are more than just beautiful. They are an important part of the natural world. They are some of the "threads" that keep the "fabric" of nature from falling apart.

Butterflies are important plant pollinators. Pollination is necessary in order for plants to produce their seeds. No seeds, no new plants! Butterflies, however, do not pollinate plants just to be nice. They are attracted to flowers to feed on their sweet nectar. Butterflies use a lot of energy when they fly. Sugar is a good source of energy for the butterfly. And nectar that is made by flowers has lots of sugar. While butterflies are feeding on flower nectar, they become dusted with the flowers' pollen. They end up carrying pollen from flower to flower while sipping nectar. The plant helps the butterfly survive, and the butterfly helps the plant survive.

Caterpillars, chrysalids, and butterflies are an important food source for many small animals.

Caterpillars, chrysalids, and butterflies are a major source of food for many animals. Caterpillars and chrysalids are eaten by mice, shrews, rats, opossums, skunks, birds, toads, scorpions, praying mantids, beetles, flies, wasps, and other insects. Butterflies are eaten by birds, some bats, lizards, monkeys, toads, spiders, dragonflies, and praying mantids. Even some plants eat butterflies! The rubber vine—or moth plant—of Australia is known to catch butterflies and moths. The Venus's-flytrap and other sundew plants of North America also catch and eat a butterfly every now and then.

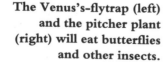

The Venus's-flytrap (left) and the pitcher plant (right) will eat butterflies and other insects.

Caterpillars eat large amounts of green plants and store the food energy in their body. This energy may be passed on to the chrysalis or butterfly. Or it may be passed on to another animal when the caterpillar is eaten. Animals that cannot eat green plants for their energy must eat animals that do eat plants. We call these animals predators, for they hunt for live prey. The smallest of these animals may become food for larger animals. The larger animals may become food for even larger animals. This connection between all living things is known as a "food web." Caterpillars are one of the most important parts of the food web, for they help so many other animals survive.

There are a few caterpillars that are predators themselves. They feed on young aphids, scale insects, leafhoppers, and ants. These smaller insects are pests, so the caterpillars that eat them are helpful to people.

Unfortunately, there are a few caterpillars that are pests themselves. The caterpillars of the mourningcloak butterfly (also known as the spiny elm caterpillar) can easily strip all the leaves off small elm and willow trees. The caterpillars of the cabbage white butterfly feed on cabbage and broccoli plants in gardens. Likewise, the caterpillars of the alfalfa butterfly can ruin a farmer's field of alfalfa. The caterpillar of the European skipper, which was accidentally brought into the United States, now causes a great deal of damage to pasture grasses.

The tomato hornworm (above) is feeding on a tomato plant. The gardener may have sprayed the plant with a chemical pest control. If that is the case, the caterpillar will probably die. If a bird were to eat the poisoned caterpillar, it would suffer. Chemical pest controls have far-reaching effects.

Caterpillars are not always welcome creatures, even though they will eventually become butterflies.

This tree has been stripped by an army of feeding caterpillars. The caterpillars are not bad, they are simply behaving the way nature intended them to behave.

41

ARE BUTTERFLIES IMPORTANT?

The Xerces blue (above) became extinct in 1944.

Pollution—all kinds—is the major reason why many butterflies are in danger.

Poisons that enter the air will eventually affect the water and the plants in the area. As certain plants become scarce, the butterflies and caterpillars that depend on them will suffer.

Not all butterflies are common. Some butterflies are so rare that their numbers can be easily counted each year. These butterflies are "endangered," meaning they may soon become extinct. When an animal or plant becomes extinct, it is gone forever! One butterfly that is now extinct is the Xerces blue. It used to live near San Francisco, California, but its habitat was destroyed by pollution and other changes. The last of these butterflies were seen in 1944. Another extinct butterfly is the Palos Verde blue. It was last seen in 1983.

There are more than 35 rare or endangered butterflies in the United States. This includes butterflies such as the Bahama swallowtail, Lange's metalmark, lotis blue, mission blue, Oregon silverspot, San Bruno elfin, Schaus' swallowtail, and Smith's blue.

Why do butterflies suffer when they lose their habitat? The main reason is the loss of their food plants. Butterflies are dependent on flowering plants for nectar, and each kind of caterpillar must eat a special kind of plant. If these special plants are no longer around, the caterpillars and butterflies are doomed.

People are responsible for most of these changes in a butterfly's habitat. Plants are destroyed by burning, plowing, logging, and construction. Native plants are often replaced by crops, pavement, or buildings. Sadly, the few butterflies that survive these changes are often killed by the poisonous chemicals used on farm fields, vegetable gardens, flower gardens, and lawns.

All the creatures that live in these North American forests will have to fight for their survival. Logging (left) and slash burning (right) are just two examples of "deforestation."

The growth in human population has destroyed butterfly habitats in many parts of the world, including habitats in your own neighborhood. Stop and think for a moment about the vacant lots, fields, and woodlands that used to be all around. Now they are housing developments or shopping malls.

One way people are helping butterflies is by protecting their habitats. Several nature organizations and governments have been trying to preserve the last remaining wintering grounds of the monarch butterfly.

Many state highway departments are turning away from costly roadside mowing and the high risks of spraying roadside weeds. Instead, they have turned their roadsides into wildflower plantings and butterfly sanctuaries! This saves money, but even better, it helps butterflies.

In nature, fewer than five percent of all butterflies reach adulthood. But raised in captivity where there is plenty of food and protection from enemies, 85 to 95 percent of the butterflies can reach adulthood! This idea of butterfly farming can help people as well as butterflies. Governments in some countries are helping their people set up butterfly farms where large numbers of butterflies are raised each year. Some of the butterflies are sold to collectors, and the rest are released into nearby butterfly habitats. In addition to earning a good living, a butterfly farmer is given a chance to earn money in a way that does not harm nature, like logging or farming in our precious rain forests.

The population is growing and the need for more housing grows with it. Are we thinking before we build?

The goal of conservation is to help nature remain in balance so that all living things have a fair chance for survival.

More and more states are planting wildflowers along their highways (above). This cuts maintenance costs, but best of all, it gives some land back to the butterflies and other creatures.

Some governments of countries that contain rain forests are helping people start butterfly farms. By farming butterflies, they are saving two precious resources at once—the butterfly and the rain forest!

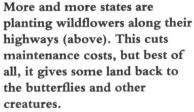

GLOSSARY

Abdomen (AB-doh-muhn): The part of the butterfly's body that holds its heart, stomach, and other organs.

Antennae (AN-ten-neye): The pair of "feelers" on an insect's head. Besides feeling, they are used for smelling and hearing.

Caddisfly (KAD-is-fleye): The winged insect from which butterflies probably evolved.

Camouflage (KAM-oh-flahj): Colors that help an animal hide in nature.

Cells (sells): The "building blocks" of which all life is formed.

Chrysalids (KRIS-uh-lidz): One of several plural forms of "chrysalis." Other plurals are "chrysalises" and "chrysalides."

Chrysalis (KRIS-uh-liss): The stage during which a caterpillar forms a shell and turns into a butterfly inside it.

Conservation (KAHN-ser-VAY-shun): The care and protection of something, often a natural resource.

Endangered species: A kind of animal or plant that is so rare it may become extinct.

Extinct: A species that is no longer living, such as the Xerces blue butterfly and dinosaurs.

Habitat (HAB-uh-tat): Where an animal lives; the special kind of environment it needs to survive.

Larva (LAR-vuh): The caterpillar stage of the butterfly.

Lepidoptera (lep-i-DOP-tuh-ruh): The order of insects that includes butterflies, moths, and skippers.

Lepidopterist (lep-i-DOP-tuh-rist): A person who studies butterflies, moths, and skippers.

Metamorphosis (met-uh-MOR-fuh-sis): A change in form. When the caterpillar changes into a butterfly, it is called metamorphosis.

Migrate (MEYE-grayt): To move from one area to another, usually over long distances.

Pollinate (PAH-luh-nayt): To carry pollen from flower to flower, leaving some pollen dust on each flower.

Proboscis (proh-BAHS-kuhs): The hollow "soda straw" tongue of the butterfly.

Pupa (PYEW-pah): The chrysalis stage of the butterfly.

Species (SPEE-shees): A group of closely related living things that are much alike and that can breed with one another in the wild.

Spiracles (SPEER-uh-kuhls): The breathing holes in the abdomen of the butterfly and caterpillar.

Thorax (THOR-aks): The middle segment of an insect's body. On a butterfly, the wings and legs are attached to the thorax.

Xerces (ZUR-seez): The name of a blue butterfly that is now extinct. The Xerces Society is a butterfly conservation group.

HOW TO SAY THESE BUTTERFLY NAMES

Admiral (AD-muh-ruhl)

Emperor (EM-per-or)

Fritillary (FRIT-uh-layr-ee)

Heliconian (HEE-lih-KOHN-ee-uhn)

Mimic (MIM-ik)

Morpho (MOR-foh)

Parnassian (par-NASS-ee-uhn)

Satyr (SAY-tur)

Sulphur (SUL-fur)

Wood nymph (wood nimf)